DMĨTRY

DMĨTRY
A YOUNG SOVIET IMMIGRANT

JOANNE E. BERNSTEIN
photographs by
MICHAEL J. BERNSTEIN

CLARION BOOKS
TICKNOR & FIELDS : A HOUGHTON MIFFLIN COMPANY
NEW YORK

For Michael   ~   For Joanne
J. B.   M. B.

Clarion Books
Ticknor & Fields, a Houghton Mifflin Company

Library of Congress Cataloging in Publication Data

Bernstein, Joanne E.
Dmitry: a young Soviet immigrant.
Summary: An account of a Soviet Jewish boy and his parents who leave present-day Moscow and resettle in the United States.
1. Jews—Russian S.F.S.R.—Moscow—Juvenile literature. 2. Jews, Russian—United States—Juvenile literature. 3. Jews—United States—Juvenile literature. 4. Soviet Union—Emigration and immigration—Juvenile literature. 5. United States—Emigration and immigration—Juvenile literature. [1. Jews. 2. Soviet Union—Emigration and immigration. 3. United States—Emigration and immigration] I. Bernstein, Michael J. II. Title.
DS135.R93M673   947'.312004924   81-2251
ISBN 0-89919-034-0   AACR2

CONTENTS

~1~
GOOD-BYE MOSCOW

Packing was the hardest. People who move from one country to another must leave most things behind. It's very hard to decide what's important to keep.

Every day two planes fly from Sheremetyevo International Airport near Moscow to Vienna. These flights bring Russian immigrants on the first leg of longer journeys. The voyages end in resettlement in other parts of the world.

Dmitry Gindin and his parents left Moscow in mid-February. They carried luggage packed with clothing, and two musical instruments—a viola and a violin. Dmitry's mother, Irina, wore a good set of earrings and a gold ring. All the other belongings had been shipped by mail to the United States. These were few: some silver spoons and a tea set, two vases, many books, boxes of sheet music, and personal papers and photographs.

Almost everything else had been sold to pay for exit visas. In order to leave Russia, people must pay the government back for some of the benefits they received over the years. The cost was 2,000 rubles for the family. In addition they had to pay 1,000 rubles in custom costs for the viola and violin.

To raise the 3,000 rubles (about $4,600 in United States currency), the Gindins sold their piano, most of Irina's clothes, and all their furniture. Dmitry says, "We had to sell everything from the bedroom, the living room, the kitchen. It was all pretty new, and very good. You can imagine how unhappy we felt. My father played viola in the Stanislavsky Opera Theatres Orchestra. He had to sell his best bow. It hurt him terribly. We didn't get the money all these things were worth. Even with everything we sold, we barely had enough money for the exit visas. But we got them. And in getting them, we gave up our Soviet citizenship."

Besides one another and their few possessions, Dmitry and his parents left Russia with about $360. With this, they hoped to make their way to the United States.

The permits given to the Gindins said that they would

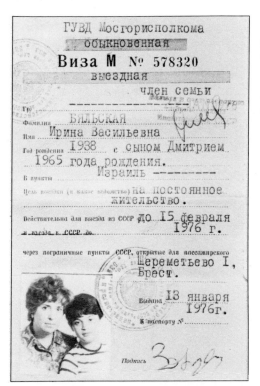

This exit visa permitted Dmitry and his mother to emigrate. His father had a separate visa.

be heading to Israel. Those who wish to emigrate from Russia receive a letter of invitation from the Israeli government. In most cases, Jews are not allowed to leave the Soviet Union unless they say they are thinking about going to Israel. In Vienna, final decisions are made.

In the past fifteen years, more than 300,000 Jews have left the Soviet Union. Dmitry came from Moscow, the capital of Russia. Russia is the largest republic of the Union of Soviet Socialist Republics. Many of the emigrants have come from Russia. Others have left other areas of the Soviet Union, especially the Ukrainian Republic.

The flight was over. Dmitry and his parents arrived in Vienna, Austria. "It smelled different immediately," Dmitry says. "It felt different. The doors in the airport opened just like *that* when you stepped on something. There was a taxi right near the door."

Immigrants are housed for a short period in Vienna. The Gindins spent ten days in a hotel.

"We were alone, in a terrible hotel, without friends," Dmitry recalls. "With us were other people from Russia. Some became friends. They now live in New York. During those days, we got our papers processed so we could go on to the next step—Italy. The Hebrew Immigrant Aid Society (HIAS) paid for our fares and expenses on the way to America. They talked to us about Israel and the other countries open to us. We thought about Israel but decided we didn't really feel Jewish enough. Most people choose either Israel or the United States, but some go to Canada, Australia, even New Zealand. We were set upon the United States. After we talked with HIAS about our plans, there was also time to see Vienna and go to museums. But it was hardly a vacation. We were so nervous."

From Vienna, immigrants go by train to Rome, where they are assigned to hotels.

It takes about four months to get papers of admittance to the United States, and even longer for Canada. The immigrants know they must learn to be comfortable in Italy for a while. HIAS sets aside money for each family's rent and provides a weekly allotment for expenses. The Gindins were given about $60 a week.

Once again, in Rome, the Gindins stayed in an inexpensive hotel. Again it was for ten days. Then, with instructions from HIAS, it was up to them to find their own furnished apartment. With the funds given them, they could afford to live only in Ostia-Lido, a community near the Mediterranean Sea about half an hour's ride from central Rome.

In Ostia-Lido, although colonies of transient Russians have become numerous, newcomers feel lost. They cannot talk with Italians in the street. They cannot read whatever they see. And they have no jobs to keep them busy.

The living allowance does not permit much luxury.

Sometimes more than one immigrant family will be forced to share an apartment. Some find they must sell some of the things they brought with them from the Soviet Union. The plaza in front of the Ostia post office has become an unofficial gathering place for immigrants. Here they find out about housing. They inquire about other families and share reactions. It is here they find out, if they should need, where to sell their jewels and silver to buy necessities.

Helping the new immigrants is a small group of older immigrants who know the Ostia-Lido area well. These are Soviet immigrants who arrived earlier and went to Israel. They later decided to leave Israel and went back to Italy, hoping to go on to the United States or other countries. When they got back to Italy, they found that in most cases they could not get into the United States or other receiving countries. This is because most Soviet immigrants are admitted under a category called "political refugees." Political refugees are thought of as people forced by oppression to leave a country. But this group of older immigrants was no longer coming from the Soviet Union. They were not forced to leave Israel, and so they are not considered political refugees.

Many Soviet immigrants, including the Gindins, are very fond of Italy and think it is a fine place to live. The immigrants who return from Israel would settle in Italy, but Italian law does not allow them to get work permits. They cannot leave, but they cannot begin to establish livelihoods. They are indeed men and women without a country. In order to survive, some have temporary jobs. Others act as representatives for newer immigrants. They help others get settled and arrange to sell things for them at the Roman flea market.

To help the Gindins prepare for going to the United States, HIAS sent Dmitry and his father to school in Rome. The two took the train and then walked half a mile to the school. There, they were taught English.

In Rome, Eduard Gindin met other Russian musicians. He also met some Italian musicians who had studied in Moscow. In a visit to a famous violin maker, Giuseppe Lucci, Eduard was introduced to other musicians who spoke no Russian. The music they shared was an international language.

Because of his fascination with ancient history, Dmitry spent hours walking around the Colosseum and other ruins of Italy's past. Dmitry also enjoyed Vatican City. St. Peter's Basilica and the Vatican Museum there were his favorites.

Besides sightseeing, Dmitry often visited Rome's plazas and arcades, where he could play with electric games.

It was expensive to play pinball and the other games, so Dmitry tried to make money. He searched for old bottles and brought them back to the store. That brought a few cents in deposit. He also tried to give drivers gas. In Rome, gas stations are self-service. Dmitry ran and tried to help out, but he was too small, and he didn't know enough Italian. There was competition from older teenagers. Dmitry kept learning more Italian and kept trying to earn money, but other young people with more experience kept pushing him out. He seldom got a chance, and this upset him, but he kept trying.

Working for money was a new experience for Dmitry. In Moscow, it's not popular for young people to earn money, and it's impossible to work until sixteen. "In Russia there is not as much entertainment to buy," says Irina. Eduard disagrees—there may not be as much entertainment, but what there is, is inexpensive. Movies are ten cents. Parents give children money as they need it. Those who live at home don't get allowance.

By May, more than three months after their arrival in Rome, the Gindins' entrance visas to the United States were ready. But they found it hard to leave Rome. Dmitry and his parents had learned some Italian. They knew what to pay for things, how to get around.

And now, just when they had to leave, the Mediterranean was more fit for swimming. In March, when the water was not as pleasant, Dmitry sampled the cold sea when he helped his young neighbor Alik out of the water. Alik had been walking from stone to stone when he fell in.

Alik and his family would be memories now. There was one other family they would not forget. The father was a mathematician. Dmitry remembers the man swam in the Mediterranean—on purpose—even in January.

On the last day in May, Dmitry and his parents flew from Rome to New York. About half of the passengers in the Boeing 747 were Soviet immigrants. The rest seemed to be Americans and Italians.

The flight usually takes about eight hours. This would have been long enough. It didn't work out that way. "The pilot announced we would be landing in ten minutes," Dmitry says. "Weather was bad, and the plane was broken. Fifteen minutes later, we left New York and started out for Boston. We skidded in to a landing. All of the immigrants sat in the plane on the ground for four hours. There was not enough air. Then we were given papers allowing us to enter the country and they put us onto another plane. What next? Another four hours on the ground doing nothing. Finally, the weather got better. By the time we took off and landed in New York, it was one o'clock in the morning. It was raining, and there were huge lights all over the place. It was scary."

On the bus trip from John F. Kennedy International Airport to Manhattan, the Gindins sat quietly. As they looked at their son, they silently asked questions they'd asked many times before: Why did we change everything to go live in rotten hotels? Why did we leave everyone and everything?

Mr. and Mrs. Gindin held excellent jobs in the Soviet

Union. Irina was an economist, helping the Soviet government analyze ways to spend its money wisely. She was an expert on fuel and energy. Her position was that of a high-level executive. Eduard had two jobs. He was a professor at the University of Moscow. There he taught and conducted a chamber orchestra. He also was a violist in the Stanislavsky Opera Theatres Orchestra.

They wondered what would happen now. They realized that in their longing they had already forgotten what it was that made them prepare for two years to leave Moscow.

As part of the preparation, Irina left her job about a year and a half before they planned to depart. She says, "If I stayed, we couldn't get permission to leave. My father was Jewish. My mother was raised as non-Jewish. Her passport, and mine too, said Ukrainian. In the Soviet Union, people carry passports the way Americans have Social Security cards. It's not for travel, but for identification. If my passport said Jewish, I couldn't have had the good position I had."

Irina left early, but Eduard worked almost until the departure date, stopping only a month before. The family was extraordinarily lucky. It took them only three months to get an exit visa. For some it takes years. "Even a lifetime," says Irina. The Soviets are reluctant to lose the services of those they have trained, and hesitate to give exit visas. Irina's brother, a scientist, still waits. In the United States he is called a *refusenik,* because his request has been denied.

Eduard's passport told everyone in the Soviet Union that he was Jewish. Jews are sometimes called *piatye punkty.* This means five-pointers. It refers to the fifth point, or question, on the passport. The question concerns nationality, and each Jew is assigned the nationality of "Jew," no matter where he or she comes from in the vast Soviet Union. Eduard says that the word Jew in Russia is a dirty word.

"This is why we left," Eduard says. Eduard thinks that most musicians in Russia are Jewish. The good job Eduard had with the University of Moscow Chamber Orchestra would now be impossible for someone like himself to get. When Eduard tried to find a replacement for himself as a conductor, he selected a man who was actually Jewish but now had a passport reading "Russian." Nevertheless, his name looked Jewish. The orchestra manager turned to him angrily, "How can you suggest this—such a terrible candidate?"

The orchestra manager didn't know Eduard was seeking to leave Russia. Eduard thinks that if he had known, Eduard would have been fired before he could resign.

In the Opera Theatres Orchestra, things were different. People there knew Eduard was leaving Russia. He needed a recommendation in order to obtain his exit visa. "I knew there they respected me," Eduard says, "so I requested the recommendation from them. They allowed me to work even though the declaration that I was leaving was a vote against the regime."

Eduard remembers the rest of the situation and his body feels cold.

"Why did we leave?" Eduard asks. "It wasn't any one thing. You ask a prisoner what he hates about prison—

what will he tell you? Most of the food in Russia was of poor quality. You couldn't predict adequate supply. Clothing quality was poor, and there were lines. But this is not enough reason to change your life totally, for food or clothes."

"No, this is something more," says Irina. "This is an expression of passive protest against the atmosphere. Even though we liked our jobs, it was no longer pleasant to go to work."

Dmitry adds, "I don't know how Russians know you are Jewish. They just know. And Jews know, even when they are young, that most of the one hundred nationalities stamped on the passports are given first-class treatment. Jews are given second class or lower. There is no official anti-Semitism on entrance tests for schools or to get certain jobs, but it is more terrible because it's not official. You depend on what other people feel like doing. Anything can happen. I guess you could say my parents left Russia because they were just fed up with everything. The political system, the social system—not being treated as we might deserve as people, not knowing what might happen next—all this made them ready to leave."

In the Soviet Union, some try to hide the fact that they are Jewish. Other Jews are not dissatisfied, and many do not wish to leave. Eduard's parents and sister, whose photos decorate the inside of his viola case, plan to stay. His sister is also a musician. His father, a member of the

Eduard's parents

Communist Party, has endured a lot over the years. He was never imprisoned in Stalin's camps, but some of his friends were. He is afraid.

Eduard's mother is a musician and a teacher of English. She understand injustices within the Russian regime. She understands the choice her son has made, but is unhappy because it is such an extreme decision. They may never see each other again. Eduard writes to his family twice a week.

19

The airport bus pulled up to a hotel in midtown Manhattan. It was June 1. Now there was no more time for thinking about why they were here. They just were.

Dmitry says of this last hotel, "We began the worst experience of our lives. It was dirty, there were roaches, and the walls and ceiling had not been painted for twenty years.

"We had never seen a room like it—the kitchen was part of the bathroom! Right next to the toilet and the shower were a stove and refrigerator. The weather was terrible, too. It was never this hot in Moscow. There was an air conditioner, but if you turned it on, the room had such a bad smell. So there was a bad choice—heat or stink.

"When we came out of the hotel in the morning, we were confused by the Empire State Building and the other tall buildings. HIAS gave us directions to the office. 'Come when you feel better or worse,' they said. The people from the New York Association for New Americans (NYANA) met with us. They gave instructions on how to look for apartments, get medical treatment, and use transportation. We were dizzy and could hardly understand. We knew we would have to visit the NYANA offices when my parents started looking for jobs.

"It took us two days to find the supermarket. We tried the hotel coffee shop but knew we would run out of money very quickly if we kept eating there. We tried to find the supermarket that first day and walked for two

hours but never found it. For two days we bought hot dogs from stands on the street.

"We were embarrassed and afraid to speak. My mother, who spoke the best, could not make her words come out clearly—she was in such shock. NYANA warned us New York was dangerous. It was so hot. And there were very strange people on the streets.

"Even though we could read numbers in English, there are so many street signs in New York City that we didn't know where to begin. We couldn't find the names we needed—Madison Avenue, Park Avenue, Broadway. There are not so many marks in Moscow. In America, there are so many parking signs and store signs. Moscow has fewer cars. It was overwhelming.

"Even when we made ourselves clear to people on the street, no one could explain where the supermarket was. Everyone in midtown lives in some other neighborhood.

"But we did find it eventually, and we had luck to find out where to buy cooking ware. For the two months we were in the hotel, we did very little. We mostly cooked our meals and went shopping. Step by step we went out, each day walking farther from the hotel. We were scared of getting lost in the big city.

"Moscow is built in a series of concentric circles. It's hard to get lost. In Manhattan, the numbered streets are easy to follow once you get the idea, but that takes time. We knew soon we'd have to go out of Manhattan, to look for an apartment by ourselves. We couldn't begin to use

22

the subway yet. We had no idea how, so we didn't go for a while.

"My mother and father attended English school while we lived in the hotel. NYANA paid for it. They paid for our hotel and food, too. I learned mostly from television. We had television in Moscow, but not so many channels. I was excited with the possibilities. After a while, though, I couldn't learn from TV all day. My father expected to audition for membership in an orchestra and he practiced five, six hours a day, even more. Sometimes I would listen to him, then I would watch TV without sound.

"Most of the time, all three of us were together. One day I will never forget. We walked from the hotel, on East 28 Street, all the way to the Metropolitan Museum of Art, which is on Fifth Avenue at 82 Street, more than three miles away. My feet were very tired, but the museum turned out to be a spectacle. I wasn't too tired to enjoy the statues and paintings. We walked back to the hotel and I could hardly pick up my feet. When we turned down East 28 Street, a drunk was lying straight across the hot sidewalk. Everything he wore was gray and brown. We had to walk around him. I thought, 'So this is America.' "

~2~
MOVING TO CANARSIE

The Gindins moved out of the hotel to an apartment on August 1. It was two months to the day from their arrival in the United States.

The eighth-floor apartment was part of Bayview, a middle-income housing project located in Canarsie. Situated alongside Jamaica Bay, Canarsie is a neighborhood in Brooklyn, one of New York City's five boroughs. Nearby is John F. Kennedy International Airport. Arriving and departing jets roar above the rooftops, frightening newcomers. Dmitry was astounded to be able to read the airlines' logos on the planes' tails from the ground.

In spite of the airplanes, the Gindins were happy to be away from the hotel. Finding a place had not been easy. In Russia, the government gets you your apartment. In fact, because there were not always enough apartments available in Moscow, at one time Dmitry and his parents shared a kitchen and bathroom with a man and his wife. They were not related to the couple. Only when Dmitry was about five years old was the government able to rent them an apartment they could have for themselves.

Now, in the United States, it was different. No gov-

25

ernment agency assigned them to an apartment. They had to look for themselves, which was hard to get used to. In the United States, if the apartment is not to your liking, you can move. In Russia, you would have to wait longer to make the change. It was all so new.

Before finding the Bayview project, the Gindins had looked at several apartments, but they were too expensive. "Or the neighborhoods weren't good," says Dmitry.

Each time the family searched for a place to live, it meant a trip on the dizzying, dirty New York subway system. The train took them by bridge or tunnel away from Manhattan, the only borough they knew at all. "After seeing the Metro in Moscow, it was very discouraging to go on the trains here. There is no comparison. The Moscow Metro is a palace, a heaven. There are statues, chandeliers, marble all over. A palace."

The rent grant the Gindins received from NYANA covered the rent at Bayview, and the neighborhood was acceptable. They took the apartment.

When Dmitry and his parents moved in, they had few possessions. They brought pots and cookware purchased in Manhattan, some crystal and the silver tea set shipped from Russia, some paintings done by Eduard, musical instruments, and clothing. Little more.

Soon they found or bought some meager used furniture. The apartment was brightened by murals painted by Dmitry and Eduard on the large walls. Magic Marker ink worked in delicately with their fingertips created soft

pastel trees and park scenes. Underneath one of the murals, Eduard had written a caption in English. It said, "Remembering Russia."

As they settled in, Dmitry and his parents tried to start a normal life.

In September Dmitry started school in the United States. It was just about a month after his move to Canarsie. "I was sent to P.S. 276 because a lot of immigrants were going there. Mrs. Seiman met me there. She's the lady who works with the Russians and helps them to learn English. NYANA told her about us, and she helped us to get our apartment, too.

"At first, I was upset. She put me in the fifth grade.

There were about the same number of kids there as there are in a Russian class—about thirty-seven. But I already had been in fifth grade in Moscow. And not one of those kids helped me in class. For a month I sat there, and it was hard. I was bigger and I knew a lot of the work.

"Some of the kids used to curse me for being Russian. Americans think Russia is their greatest enemy. Their parents tell them that, so the kids curse. That's when I first started thinking about changing my name to Jim or Dean. My name at home is Dima. That sounds like Jim and Dmitry sounds like Dean, don't you think?

"One time when I was cursed, I just punched someone, but sometimes I didn't do anything. Mostly they did it to the younger boys. They knew I was strong and they were younger.

"In fifth grade I noticed that the kids didn't stand to speak. And they raised their hands differently. In Moscow, you sit with one arm folded in front of you. You put your other elbow on the table, with that arm up. To put your arm up all the way is unmannerly.

"In this class in P.S. 276, there was no commander. In Moscow, someone is elected at the beginning of the year. That student is best in everything and stays commander if he or she continues to be best. Most commanders are girls. The commander watches others, marks tests, and speaks for the class when the class has decided something.

"By October, I was promoted to sixth grade. Here the teacher was very nice and so was the class. I still went to Mrs. Seiman to study English. She told me to take English books out of the school library for book reports. The first one I did was on a kids' book called *Snow*. It took ten minutes. It was real easy. The last one I did at the end of sixth grade was *Tales from the Thousand and One Nights*.

"With Mrs. Seiman, I always knew I had someone I can talk with. When I didn't understand something, I took the paper to Mrs. Seiman and she explained. But my teacher didn't like it—the wise guy likes to spend time somewhere else.

"I was amazed to see how little work American children do. The school day in Russia is shorter—from 8:30 to 1:30. But in Russia, you go six days, and always you do something. Here they waste time. Here, you forget homework, you say 'I forgot.' You won't forget next time in Russia. You can't goof off. To get to University it takes *some* brain. It's free, so it's very hard to get in.

"By the time I left Moscow, I had three hours of homework a night. By fourth grade, my parents couldn't always do my mathematics homework right away. Here is an example I might have. It's not the hardest:

A cat is running 5 kilometers per hour. A dog starts chasing 15 minutes later, at a speed of 8 kilometers per hour. How long will it take him to catch up?

"The teachers move children's brains to think. My brain could never solve those problems now."

30

Dmitry noticed other differences between Soviet and American schools. "Education and children are more important in Russia. Children are called the privileged class. Children's things are sold in special stores. These stores are filled with merchandise when others are not. The University of Moscow built its science building in the form of a tower. Its tallness shows everyone how important it is to do as Lenin said. He said we must study, study, study."

Dmitry's schooling began when he was one year old. Until he was two he went to day nursery. He attended six days a week, while his parents worked. In Russia, many women stay home for a few months before and after the birth of a child. They are paid. If they want to stay home longer, they will not be paid. Their jobs will be waiting for them when they want to return. Often, they return to work. Because women retire at age fifty-five in the Soviet

Dmitry as a six-month-old baby

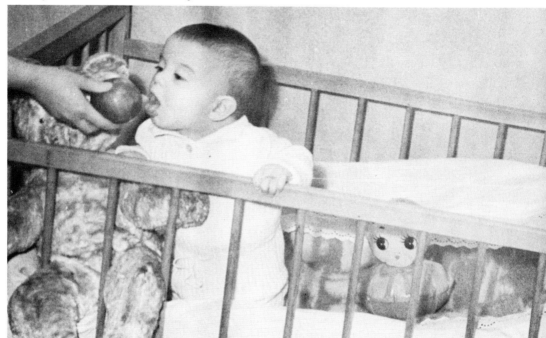

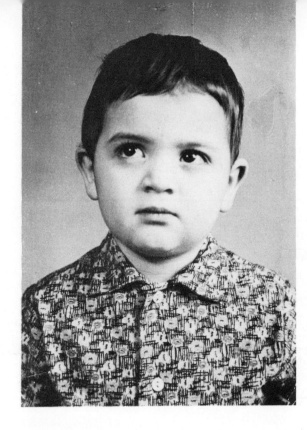

Dmitry attended a nursery from ages one through four. OPPOSITE: He is seated in the first row, on the far right.

Union, many children stay with a *babushka* (grandmother) while their mothers work. Others go to nursery. The government will sometimes pay for part or all of the cost.

At two, Dmitry switched to a nursery where he slept over all weeknights, going home only for weekends. Five people, called upbringers, took care of ten children in a group. "It was a special, elite nursery," Dmitry's mother says. "Mostly children of performing artists went there. The parents were opera singers, musicians, actors. The children played games, looked at books, had musical lessons, and learned to take care of themselves."

At five, Dmitry went to kindergarten. He began kin-

32

dergarten, still sleeping away, in the wooded coun-
tryside. His father's union helped to pay expenses, and
this school also was attended by artists' children. But
then the kindergarten closed. Dmitry returned to the out-
skirts of Moscow. Now he slept alongside the children of
people who worked in economics with his mother. This
was an international group—children from Mongolia,
Hungary, and Poland were there along with Russians.

Dmitry's mother remembers. "You can see how Russians feel about children. At the kindergarten, Dmitry ate
good food—caviar, fresh fruit. For children, the government saved things their parents couldn't buy in the
stores."

In first grade, Dmitry began staying home at night with his parents in their Moscow apartment. School begins on September 1 each year. *Every* year, Soviet children bring bouquets to the teacher on that day. They look forward to returning to school. In first grade, though, there is a special celebration called "First Time in First Class." All the friends and relatives of the new students accompany them to school, cheering them on. The day is celebrated on TV and in the newspaper, too, with programs and articles about the importance of learning.

Dmitry had the same small, plump woman as his teacher from first grade through third grade. "The teacher is the second mother in elementary school. You come to her and ask everything. She teaches most subjects. In fourth grade, you get different teachers for different subjects. This is called Middle School. By sixth grade, you learn physics. In seventh, you learn chemistry."

Parents in Moscow can choose from several schools for their children. Dmitry's school was special because he began learning English as a foreign language in second grade. If he'd stayed until seventh grade, some subjects, such as British and American literature and British and American history, would have been taught not in Russian but in English.

It seems to the Gindins that more classic reading material is studied in Russia than in the United States. Adults spark their conversations with quotations from authors, and children do too. There is greater emphasis upon reading certain books. Children read Russian authors (Leo Tolstoi, Feodor Dostoevski, Aleksandr Pushkin, and others) and books about Russian history. Young people feel that authors such as Charles Dickens, Mark Twain, and Jack London are musts. Books such as *The Three Musketeers* and *The Wizard of Oz* are popular.

Dmitry also finds differences in family life between Russia and the United States. "School is not the only thing that is different here. Parents are different with their children, too. Even with babies. Russian babies are carried much more. They are breast-fed more. And more mothers are at work in Russia. Women work at everything, even with ax in hand.

"Both parents are in charge of the children. Because the mother is away, children grow up faster. When I was seven, I had a key to my apartment. Sometimes my father was there when I got home from school. Other times I stayed by myself in the afternoon. I got dinner warm. Sometimes my father did two performances in one day. He would leave at six or seven for the evening performance. My mother didn't come home until eight.

"If I had brothers or sisters, they would help me with dinner, but it's not unusual for a family in Moscow to have only one child. Families in the United States are bigger. In Moscow, almost no one has more than two kids. It would be hard to feed them."

Young people in Russia and the United States are similar in the things they do after school. In both countries many go to community centers or take lessons of one kind or another. In Russia, children may spend time at an after-school center, playing games or taking lessons. Activities range from gymnastics to chess, just as in the United States.

For most of his after-school activity in Russia, Dmitry attended the Prokofiev Music School. It was a museum as well as a school. The desk and piano of Sergei Prokofiev, the composer of *Peter and the Wolf,* were on permanent display. Two days a week, for two hours a day, Dmitry studied violin and sang in a choir.

In Canarsie, Dmitry didn't take music lessons. He practiced sometimes at home. And if he visited a place where there was a piano, he plunked out the melodies he'd played on violin.

Dmitry did not miss the music lessons, but he did yearn for the outdoor activities he enjoyed in Moscow. Although he swam at a community center in Canarsie almost every day, the activity was indoors.

"In Russia, people think it's important to go outside every day. Soccer, basketball, hockey we played. One of the games I liked best is called *durak.* Translated, it means idiot, or stupid. You take a soccer ball and get a line of kids. As many as you want. The first guy kicks the ball against a wall. It can only touch the wall once. Then the next on line must kick it. The line keeps going around. If you miss once, you get a *D.* The next time you get a *U.* If you spell *durak,* you are out."

In winter Russians still spend time each day outdoors. "I like cross-country skiing. Americans think Moscow is terribly cold. They have it mixed up with Siberia. It's really very nice," Dmitry says. Actually, Moscow is no colder in winter than Minnesota or parts of New England.

Dmitry feels some Americans have other false ideas

about Russia. He wants those he meets to know that Russians have refrigerators, stoves, and television. "Some Americans think Russians are cave people."

But Dmitry also had false impressions of America, he found. "I never imagined it was so hard to get a job here. And I thought that in America there was no discrimination against people. But now I see that I was wrong."

Dmitry's months in Canarsie were filled with going to school and observing his surroundings. His father's months in Canarsie were filled with frustration. Soon after leaving the hotel in Manhattan, he managed to arrange an audition for a job in music. "It was a job as violist with the St. Louis Symphony. I played well, but they didn't accept me."

As soon as he returned from St. Louis, Mr. Gindin began preparing for his next audition. He always had to be at his best. Eduard tried out for several orchestras, including symphonies in Boston, Baltimore, and North Carolina. When he had to travel to an audition, an organization called the American Council for Emigres in the Professions helped to pay his fare.

But at all the interviews, the answer was the same—no.

Mr. Gindin remembers that as the months wore on, his mood got worse. "Having no job was a punch to my future," he says.

There were a few opportunities to play music, but they didn't pay much money. One such chance came through

a professor from Sarah Lawrence College named Joel Spiegelman, who had spent several years in Moscow studying harpsichord.

Dmitry tells about Spiegelman's idea. "He wanted to start a Russian Chamber Orchestra in New York City—only immigrants. My father was so excited when he was accepted, especially because he and Spiegelman graduated from the Gnesin School at the same time. But the chamber orchestra couldn't be a regular job, just concerts from time to time. You can't live on that. My father wanted a permanent job, so he kept practicing."

During the months he practiced and played with the Russian Chamber Orchestra, Eduard Gindin also played with the American Symphony Orchestra. But he was a substitute and was called only if someone was sick. There was no way to rely upon a paycheck.

Through it all, NYANA kept calling to remind Eduard to get a job. "They didn't want to keep paying for our rent and food," Dmitry says. "But what did they expect, a man like my father to wash dishes? To prostitute himself?"

In Canarsie, NYANA paid for the family's food for six months. They paid the apartment rent for ten months.

Irina Gindin was sent by NYANA to an accounting course. "It was to retrain European professionals. For the sixteen weeks I took the course, I got some money which we needed, so I went. But the level of training was very low—like an assistant bookkeeper. It was ridiculous. One man in the course had been a philologist in Russia. Imagine this man, a well-known scholar of languages, wasting his time for four months. Should all his training go down the drain?"

In the spring, after more than half a year in Canarsie, Irina got a job doing economic analysis for a bank. It was a temporary job, just for a few months, but Irina thought it was a beginning.

Finally, in May, Eduard tried out at an audition and was a success. He was given a one-year contract to play viola in the Syracuse Symphony in upstate New York!

The Gindins made plans for the fall. Eduard would live

for the year in Syracuse, 250 miles away. Irina and Dmitry would move back to Manhattan, where they had reserved an apartment in a new tower that was being built to house performing artists and their families. The performer in the Gindin family would be away, but they looked ahead with hope. Irina's job in the bank would soon end, but there would surely be another. They all said, "It is only for a year."

~3~
SYRACUSE

The summer was not easy. Since Mr. Gindin's full-time job would not begin until September, he found a summer job at a music camp called Merrywood, near Lee, Massachusetts. For a small sum, he taught viola to children. They, in turn, enriched his English.

Dmitry was sent to a sleepaway camp by a Jewish charity. He hated it. There were too many regulations. They did the same activities again and again, and he didn't like the kids. Once, some kids stripped his bed and hid all his bed linen.

Meantime, his mother spent another hot summer in New York. It was worse than before. She was alone in Canarsie, without a job, without friends, and without her family. The loneliness the three Gindins suffered in those forty-five days convinced them they must not separate in the fall as they had planned.

As soon as Dmitry and his father returned from their camps, his mother was dispatched on the five-hour trip to Syracuse. "You will find an apartment, while we get ready to move," said Eduard.

Irina found an apartment just one block from the

downtown Civic Center where the Syracuse Symphony rehearses and plays. It was part of an apartment-house complex, three imposing twenty-story towers called Presidential Plaza. The most luxurious apartments were named for Thomas Jefferson, middle-income apartments for James Madison. Low-income families, mostly senior citizens, lived in the building named for William Harrison.

Confident that she would soon get a job, Irina Gindin took an apartment in Madison Manor. Calling home to Canarsie, she said, "Take everything."

The money Eduard had earned at Merrywood went for a deposit. Now the problem was finding money to move. One Russian family gave them $100 and an American man lent them another $100. This was enough to rent a small truck and make the move. Besides the $200, Dmitry and Eduard had only $5. And this had to last for six days. To save money, the two walked for almost two hours to reserve the truck at the rental company.

Dmitry can still repeat the route. From their Bayview apartment on Seaview Avenue, down Rockaway Parkway to Flatlands, and on and on and on Flatlands (or is it Flatfeet?) until Kings Highway.

The truck was reserved, a deposit of $10 left. Then, after walking all the way back home, Eduard found out that although his international driver's license was valid, it was a crime to drive a truck without previous American experience. Back they went to get the deposit. Before a satisfactory arrangement was made, Dmitry and his father made four walking trips back and forth to the Kings Highway truck rental agency.

At last an acquaintance volunteered to drive them in his car, with a trailer attached. Eduard emptied the apartment himself. After the modern furniture they'd had in Moscow, it humiliated Dmitry to carry old, dirty mattresses and furniture. Eduard understood and brought most things down himself.

After the move to Syracuse, Eduard began work with the Syracuse Symphony. But Irina could not get a job. She became a volunteer in a research project at Syracuse University, studying the economic system of the Soviet Union. It never led to a job offer, and the Gindins were disappointed.

As time went on, they realized their hopes hadn't come to pass and that most of Eduard's salary was going for rent in Madison Manor. They arranged to move into Harrison House, the least expensive of the towers in Presidential Plaza. This time the family had the needed experience but no truck was required—most of the move was made by countless trips with a folding shopping cart.

The four-room apartment in Harrison House was both more and less than what they'd had in Moscow. In Moscow, Dmitry slept in the living room. Dmitry jokes, "Do you know that if two guests came to visit us in Moscow, one would have to stay in the bathroom?"

There was little furniture in the new apartment—mattresses on the floor, a dinette table. Most books and clothing were in boxes stored in closets and on the floor.

"Once," Dmitry's father tells, "there was a chance to get more furniture. We still lived in Madison Manor. Someone threw out two old mattresses, which could have been used as a living room couch. We looked at them. 'Should we take them? What will people think?' We circled around them all day, trying to decide. Luckily, after six o'clock, they disappeared."

Soon after the move to Syracuse, Dmitry started seventh grade at Lincoln Junior High School, just a few blocks from Presidential Plaza. "The teachers were fine, but the program was very low. They were doing fractions in math, and they had no books. The only part of the program I liked was art. I brought in an oil painting of autumn trees which my father and I did together. Sometimes we stay up until two in the morning, painting. But art is not all of school. I couldn't stand the rest."

Dmitry was allowed to take the admittance test for the Manlius Pebble Hill School, an expensive private school. He passed, and was very proud. Another Russian boy he knew—a good instrumentalist—was not admitted. It would have been very hard for the family to send him, but Dmitry got a scholarship.

Dmitry liked the Manlius Pebble Hill School much better. "Even here, some of the math we were doing I learned in Moscow. But I started to learn French, and in social studies it was interesting. In phys ed there are basketball, Ping-Pong, and other sports. And I hope to play soccer."

Sports are important to Dmitry. In Syracuse, he missed very few things about New York City—the library, the Metropolitan Museum of Art, a park near his house in Canarsie. But what he really missed was the community center. Almost every day he had gone swimming, played pool and basketball, and lifted weights. There was no center in Syracuse. Besides gym in school, Dmitry occasionally borrowed a ten-speed bicycle from Lindsay, a cellist in the Syracuse Symphony orchestra. He wanted to take an overnight bicycle trip in the Syracuse area in the summer. But that was not enough.

Without a place to go each day after school, Dmitry

missed his good friends from Moscow even more than he had in New York. There were two, Alexander and Andy.

"Alexander was my friend from music school, a friend always, from the time I was very small. He never got into trouble. We went to a lot of movies together. In Russia, children go alone to movies, starting when they are about ten. Here, I almost never go. Alexander has one habit, though. He thinks everyone will never leave him even if he's inconsiderate.

"Andy likes to get into trouble. He likes chewing gum best of all. All Russian children like it. It's not made in the Soviet Union, because people say you look like a cow when you chew it. So children are happy when they can get it. Once, Andy also smoked. I see twelve-year-olds smoking here. If you did it in Russia and someone noticed, it would be embarrassing. The police might be called. They would take you and call your parents.

"I missed these two friends. They're still in Russia."

Dmitry's parents also felt nostalgia for their life in Russia, especially when letters arrived.

As the Gindins settled in, they wrote home often and received frequent letters from their friends and relatives in Russia. Within a month, everyone in Moscow knew what was going on with the Gindins. In return, Dmitry and his parents quickly learned what had happened to their friends who remained in Russia and to those who had left for other destinations.

Dmitry and his mother Irina read at the dinette table. Often Dmitry's father came in from shopping and, without removing his coat or saying a word, joined them, opening letters and devouring the news. Once Dmitry received a letter from an old Russian friend of the family.

Now living in Toronto, she included a Canadian twenty-dollar bill with her letter. "What will you buy?" asked his mother. "I will probably buy nothing," Dmitry answered. "I will save it in a collection."

Another time, Eduard also received something to save. A member of the University of Moscow Chamber Orchestra sent a photo of the group that had appeared in the newspaper. Eduard closely studied the face of the man who replaced him as conductor. Then he folded the picture carefully and placed it back in the envelope. Usually when the three finished reading their own mail, they exchanged letters and started in once again.

Softly, Irina says, "Letters bring me big nostalgia. That is my illness, I fear."

The Gindins felt that Syracuse was different from Moscow and New York. Dmitry thought the people were friendlier. "In New York, more kids will come up to you—'Hey, you want a punch in the nose?' You say 'No.' They say 'Okay, you get one anyway.' "

The people may be more welcoming. The weather, a frequent topic of conversation in that blustering upstate New York city, is not.

Syracuse weather rarely cooperates with the human urge toward joy. Sheets of rain relentlessly pound at the Gindins' window. Other times, it's the depressing *tzz-tzz* of a drizzle. For more than four months of the year, harsh snow blankets the city, rapidly turning new cars into old.

And almost always, furious winds make travel a challenge.

The city's name reminded Dmitry of its Russian translation. *Syeri* means gray in Russian. Undaunted though, he quips, "You cannot expect to see the sun *every* year." For Dmitry's father, the city of 200,000 was a reflection of himself. "I'm small and quiet like Syracuse, and sad, like the weather."

Even without sun, Dmitry was glad to be in Syracuse. There were no good friends in New York City. Perhaps, in time, more would be here. Also, Dmitry preferred not to be among so many immigrants. Half of those Russians who emigrate to the United States settle in the New York City area.

After several months, Dmitry's parents bought a car, their first ever. For Dmitry, it was a dream come true. Without the car, Mr. Gindin could not get Dmitry over to the Manlius Pebble Hill School, which is in the suburbs. "The school is in a good neighborhood, much better than Canarsie or downtown Syracuse."

The Gindins hoped that one day the car would be a link to new friends. At the beginning, though, it was exciting just to sit in it, to take it shopping, to drive out to Green Lakes, a state park. Dmitry noticed that his father could not drive and follow signs at the same time, so Dmitry became the navigator. He read maps and street signs and gave directions.

Dmitry watched the way people drove—their posture, where they put their hands on the wheel, if their knuckles turned white with tension. On private property, where it was safe, with his father's help he taught himself how to drive. "I trusted him," says Eduard, "and he appreciated that."

Mrs. Gindin planned to take her written test for the learner's permit. The three of them enjoyed making fun of the formal language in the rule book. Certain questions

began, "Under what circumstances is it permitted . . ."
They made up: "to fall asleep while driving?" The answer
was "When the road is straight."

The car helped the family get some of the foods they
favor. "Milk foods are not tasty here because they are not
natural. Yogurt, cottage cheese, sour cream, they are all
different here. Raw milk we can get in Syracuse, but it
still doesn't have the deep taste of milk in the Soviet
Union. My mother says I look like a big, fat cat. I love
good milk," Dmitry says.

The car was helpful, but it added to the bills. The family still owed money to HIAS and NYANA, the organizations that brought them here. And, even with Dmitry's scholarship, the school sent bills to the house—for books, for lunches, for this and that. There was no money to buy furniture, and they hoped no one would need a doctor or dentist. "In the Soviet Union, you cannot get along without a job," says Mrs. Gindin. "Here, you cannot get along without money. Lots of money."

In Russia, Dmitry did not learn about Jewish holidays and customs. He was not interested in being religious or learning about Judaism, but in the United States he grew interested in reading about the history of the Jews, particularly Jews in antiquity.

At the same time, Dmitry realized he was glad to be in the United States as a Jew. "Here I have a chance to do something. I was not able to do as much there because I was a Jew. You wouldn't like it if someone would call you kikeface. It didn't happen to me because I don't look Jewish, but it would be harder to get a good job or get into University."

Struggling to feel at home, Dmitry and his parents were always interested in what other immigrants—from Russia, and other countries too—were doing, and how they were feeling. They heard news of some Russians they knew in Rome and Canarsie. One, a doctor in the Soviet Union, now owned a gas station. A construction engineer had become a taxi driver. One woman continued working in her field. In Russia, she was a harpist for the Riga Symphony Orchestra. Now she was the substitute harpist for a show in New York City, *The Fantasticks.* She was happy to get the work. She estimated there were two thousand professional harpists in the United States. Many of them were in New York, she felt, all competing for the same jobs.

For Dmitry's mother, the search for work continued. Unwilling to do bookkeeping, she tried to get accounting work, although this was not the best use of her knowledge. Lindsay, their cellist friend, tried to help in getting a job.

Time was spent thinking of the future and the improvements it would bring. Dmitry's grandmother—Irina's mother—was now in Rome, waiting for her visa to come to the United States. A homemaker in the Soviet Union, Dmitry's modern, up-to-date grandmother would love some of the American conveniences, Dmitry thought. Dmitry wrote to her, explaining what she could look forward to, and adding notes on how to get from Ostia to the Villa Borghese and other places in Rome. Irina would be less lonely when her mother arrived. They all would.

There were several Russian families in Syracuse, including one musician Eduard knew in Moscow. These people were pleasant, but with most they had little in common besides the recent journey. With one family they

55

planned to celebrate New Year's Eve, breaking open champagne at midnight. They hoped to have a New Year's tree. The tree is decorated like the American Christmas tree, but there is no Christmas celebration in the Soviet Union, only New Year's. "It is nice to be with others on New Year's Eve, but it is not the same as having family nearby."

Family and a good job make the difference as to whether an immigrant is happy or not. Dmitry was more contented in Syracuse because his father suffered less there. Mr. Gindin felt he would be happy to stay in Syracuse for a long, long time. "I wanted to start a chamber orchestra in Syracuse. That was my purpose," he says.

Eduard Gindin often sat crosslegged on the small rug in his bare living room. He talked with his son of the frustration he had felt a few months before without a job. Dmitry recalled, "You did nothing very different because you did not work. You were still my father." Mr. Gindin's eyes would be far away as both remembered the different mood of just a few months earlier.

But Irina Gindin still had little to smile about. In the Soviet Union, even more than in the United States, what you do is what you are. Irina felt that work of all kinds and at all levels was given more dignity and importance there. When she could not find a job in America, part of her good feelings about herself were gone.

Mrs. Gindin says, "It is very hard to start everything all over. We lost everything. We lost not only jobs but a

culture. In America I had it only inside. There, everything was around us. Now we were like babies, starting all over. We were without roots. We were like plants without soil. I was not living, merely existing. My soul was dying.

"Sometimes I believed it was a bad dream. I felt sorry for my age. I hadn't that much future. We wanted to give knowledge and culture to society, but no job was available for me."

But each of the Gindins knew that no matter how hard it became in America for any one of them, there was no going back to Russia. "If we asked to go back, we would get an apartment, but not the same jobs. We would be asked to go on TV and radio to speak of our disappointment. And who knows what would happen in one or two years?"

57

~4~

SYRACUSE TODAY

"Hello . . . I was practicing, but I can stop. Okay, I'll meet you in fifteen minutes. Good-bye."

Dmitry hangs up and rushes to replace his violin in its case. These days Dmitry practices a lot, sometimes three or four hours a day. Still, music takes second place to being with people, and as soon as Peter calls, Dmitry is ready to dash off.

A year has passed since the Gindins moved to Syracuse. During his first full year in the city, Dmitry has met several friends, but Peter Kosoff is his favorite.

"He's in my class. We spend afternoons together. He's got a good sense of humor. In fact, he plays tricks more often than I do," Dmitry says with a smile.

The two visit one another frequently, traveling by bicycle. Some of the money for Dmitry's used ten-speed bike came from his own earnings. During the spring and summer, he and Peter helped Peter's father with the gardening around his house. Dmitry also watched the Kosoffs' dogs when the family went on vacation.

Dmitry is proud of his cycling ability, especially the fact that he is able to climb the steep hills on the route to

Peter's house. "You think this is easy? It's not. Try it if you think it is."

Set at the crest of the last hill, following a slope of stately homes, is Peter's home. Designed by his father, an architect, it is a modern home that reflects both the Kosoffs' material comfort and casual style of living.

Dmitry's parents are pleased that the Kosoffs have not

let their wealth keep them from welcoming those who are not wealthy. Mrs. Gindin says, "Dmitry finds them interesting, and they find him interesting as well. It is simple to communicate with them. The parents make jokes and so does their son."

"The other day we were playing soccer in his driveway," Dmitry recalls. "The ball rolled all the way down

61

that long hill. I ran down to get it. It took a few minutes until I came back up. Peter was waiting calmly. He saw me and said, 'While you're doing all that "Russian" around, do you mind if I kick the ball down the hill again?' "

Fist on chin, Dmitry pauses to reflect. "Peter is more athletic than I am. But I'm better in volleyball and soccer. I got him interested in soccer. Now he thinks it's great."

Mr. Gindin comments, "Dmitry realized that the thinner, stronger boy could move better in athletics. He wants to be attractive, so he has stopped buying sweet things. As you can see, he looks like he's going to be a man soon.

"Dmitry and Peter try to get me to join in their athletics. I used to play volleyball very well in my youth. I stopped, though. It is no good for the fingers with a viola.

"Dmitry has brought me into soccer. I enjoy that with the boys—my hands are safe there. Bike riding is not bad for the hands, but I'm not sure I want to do it with them. They took me eight–nine miles to Green Lakes. I couldn't walk well after that. I fear it's too late for me.

"Peter and Lindsay are better company for him on the bicycle. This past summer, Dmitry and Lindsay took a thirty-five-mile bike ride—to West Amboy, New York."

"It took five hours," Dmitry says. "We went fairly fast. It was very hilly in one place—for over an hour, up and down. At one point a dog ran after me, barking. That kept me going pretty fast, too. I made only one mistake. We

stopped to eat and I had steak. It takes energy to digest a steak, and I didn't have energy for the ride after that."

Each month that passes enables the Gindins to afford more and to live better. At the end of their first year, Eduard's symphony contract was renewed. The number of his private students is growing. Now bit by bit they are buying some of the things they need.

The first car they bought had two fires, so there is a new car. "The engine seemed to be burning out, so we traded it in before it got serious," says Dmitry. "We got something better, a Malibu."

Their apartment sports new, modern furniture, mixed with attractive used pieces they have picked up. Coordinated lamps and tables decorated with cork and aluminum gleam in the living room. At center stage is a new stereo set, filling the house with classical music recorded in Russia and the United States.

Framed drawings of Merrywood dot the walls, punctuating the improvements in their apartment. The Gindins face a better view when they look out, also. After about a year on the twelfth floor, still moving upward, they changed to the seventeenth level. This apartment has the same number of rooms, but a different arrangement makes them seem more spacious. More important, the windows are not directly over an ever-busy highway, so there is less noise.

The family travels more now: occasional trips to Canada (to see the woman who gave Dmitry the twenty-dollar bill); a trip to New York City (to see about jobs for Irina); a trip to the Tanglewood Music Festival (to see a Russian conductor who had emigrated to Israel and was on tour in the United States). Once, Dmitry and his family got together with Peter and his folks for a visit to the Thousand Islands area of New York.

"We had such a good time, laughing about silly things," Dmitry recalls. "One time, a storekeeper was trying to sell us something. First he wanted five dollars, then three. Finally he said, 'Look, I'll pay you three dollars to take it away.'"

At times, Dmitry's parents travel without him. They've gone to Canada and Niagara Falls, leaving Dmitry in Syracuse. When they are traveling, Dmitry either visits friends or stays in the apartment alone.

While there is furniture, a car, and occasional travel, there still isn't enough money for the Gindins to simply go out and buy whatever they'd like. Some of their purchases are made on time payments, and, like all families in time of inflation, they try to cut corners. On the trip to Tanglewood, for example, Dmitry and his father didn't stay overnight, but drove six hours back to Syracuse instead.

As with everything else, Dmitry jokes about expenses. In autumn a friend notices that he will need a new jacket in a couple of months, for the one he wears is getting small. Dmitry quips, "This will last. I never grow in winter."

During this year in Syracuse, the family's thoughts about Russia have changed. They still miss their homeland and make efforts to see other Russians, particularly musicians, but they make fewer comparisons. When they do compare, they are increasingly pleased with what they find in America.

Dmitry tells it this way, "Now that I know more English, I have a lot in common with kids here. They talk to me more. It feels good to understand everything kids my age understand. Before, I was jealous that my desk partners understood the books in school.

"My accent has improved. I used to say 'dat.' Now I say 'that.' My parents speak better English, too. They both read books in English and my father gives violin lessons in English. Also, my father writes to his mother in English now. She is proud because she teaches English in the Soviet Union."

Dmitry sometimes teaches his father new words, but once in a while Eduard would be better off without his son's help. "Dmitry told me a word. I asked my student what it meant and found out it was a dirty word."

Like many Russian immigrants, the Gindins try to be precise in their use of English. They listen carefully and mentally catalog each new word they hear. A friend asks Dmitry to forgive the debris in her car. Dmitry replies with excitement: "Debris! I just learned that word. It means accumulated junk and garbage!"

Knowing both Russian and English has helped Dmitry

with his eighth-grade French. "I can pick it up a little better. The alphabet is similar to English. And it's like Russian because it has feminine and masculine words and formal and informal constructions."

With greater skill in English, Dmitry understands more about the American lifestyle. "I see that American families do things more—play games, go on picnics, eat out. In Russia, my parents and I went to the woods for pleasure a lot. We still do that here, but the standard of living is higher here. It would be hard to go back down again. In Russia you stand on line for food and clothing. A car and house cost a lot in relation to salary."

Dmitry's happiness is proven in his responses to remarks about Syracuse. One visitor from New York City, noting Syracuse's blue taxis and yellow fire trucks, comments, "What a mixed-up town."

Dmitry retorts, "You mean New York?"

Likewise, Dmitry won't let outsiders attack the weather. "I like it," he announces loyally. Being loyal doesn't mean that he is not curious, however, and seeing the October snow flurries settle on cars seventeen stories below, he dashes to the telephone. He dials the weather bureau, an American habit he has picked up. There is a busy signal. Ten minutes later the phone rings. Delighted, Dmitry jokes, "See? The weather bureau is calling *us.*"

The Gindins are pleased with the friendships they are beginning to form. Lindsay still visits, although she is

busy practicing to audition for the job as first cellist in the Syracuse orchestra. Fred, a neighbor in Presidential Plaza, seems anxious to get to know them. And Eduard's music students have become companions.

One family, the Monkmans, has welcomed the Gindins eagerly. The father is a musician and Eduard teaches the teenaged daughters, Sarah and Margaret. The girls take their lessons at the Gindins' house. They frequently join in family meals or linger to kid around with Dmitry.

The Gindins have visited the Monkman farm, thirty-five miles from Syracuse. In the summer, when his parents traveled, Dmitry stayed over, enjoying the comfortable atmosphere of their larger family.

Margaret and Sarah play in the youth chamber group Eduard has formed, and are very serious about their music. "Do you know what their father once did?" asks Eduard, his eyebrows rising. "He was working in the same building where we were rehearsing. But then he forgot Sarah and Margaret and went home without them. He had to come all the way back. The man has six children and I guess it's hard to remember them all!"

The Gindins are intensely interested in American culture and American writing. One American author the Gindins especially admire is Irving Stone. Dmitry and his parents have read several of his books about artists, including *The Agony and the Ecstasy* (about Michelangelo) and *Lust for Life* (about Vincent van Gogh). They are drawn to biographies of painters because they, too, have gained their income from the arts. Dmitry and his parents also enjoyed W. Somerset Maugham's book about Paul Gauguin, *The Moon and Sixpence*.

"Van Gogh's teacher said that to be a great painter, you have to suffer all your life," Dmitry recalls. "My father, too, has suffered. People don't always appreciate performers during their lives. Like a car, once it's gone—then you appreciate it.

"In music, as in painting, there is very big competition. You must have a strong nervous system for auditions. I won't become a violinist for this reason. The same thing with drawing. In school I am known as an artist and my pictures hang in the dean's office. (Funny—last year I did buildings. This year I draw girls.) But I will draw only for recreation. I don't want to live the way my father has. Each picture takes at least three hours and some are done again and again. One oil painting I gave to Sarah."

Artists of all kinds are discussed frequently in the Gindin household. Eduard saves stamps with beautiful artwork. "I had a big collection in Russia, but they wouldn't let me take it." Finger pointing to his temple, Eduard shakes his head. "Smart."

Eduard has part of his art collection, however. "I got to take these prints. This art is by Feodor Vasiliev. He died young—in his twenties—and was unappreciated in his life. Now he has greater esteem."

Eduard says that his youth orchestra has given him the sense of purpose he needs. "There are not too many students yet. Playing in a group is like trying a new food. You have to taste and see if it's all right for your stomach. My students already have deep feeling. The orchestra will grow. We are looking for grants to support the work.

"Dmitry started to hear nice sounds the students quickly produced. This prompted him to practice. He plays in the school orchestra and was given a violin award."

"Sometimes I play with my father's students," Dmitry confides. "I don't want to be professional, but why should I waste my capabilities?"

Dmitry has his school, and Eduard has his music, but for Irina the days are less full. When asked what has been happening, she turns inward and smiles.

"Nothing has happened. Absolutely nothing," she says.

Irina has continued to look for a job, but she has been overqualified for almost everything available. "There was only one good job offer, but it was in Canada. There was a position in Toronto at the Institute for Political Analysis. It was a good job, but I didn't want to emigrate."

Mrs. Gindin still hopes for something worthwhile in the United States. "I go to the University to get the college paper. I keep looking. I plan to see a Sovietologist at Harvard about possibilities, and next week I will take a state civil service examination for a research position.

"I'm concerned about such tests. In the USSR, there are few tests. Instead, students mostly have conversations with professors. It's possible to pass a test and not know anything. Talking with a teacher, it's impossible to hide."

Irina also plans to apply for government and foundation grants. She wants to help develop balance-of-payment projects for Eastern European countries.

While she waits, Mrs. Gindin tries to keep busy. "I read a lot, and spend time with my mother."

Irina passed her driver's test on the first go-round, an admirable accomplishment.

"I'm a good teacher," her husband chuckles.

With the new family car, Mrs. Gindin can drive to see some Russian friends she has met. "My mother and I see them about twice a week. It is good for me. We enjoy each other's company, and we speak Russian."

Anna Byalskay, Mrs. Gindin's mother, arrived in the United States in February. After landing at Kennedy airport and staying in New York City overnight, she joined the Gindins in Syracuse.

The trip to the United States had not been as pleasant as Mrs. Byalskay had hoped. Unlike her daugher, she did not enjoy Italy. But now she was glad to begin to settle down.

For one month, Mrs. Byalskay lived with the Gindins in their four-room apartment. At that point, she was able to get a one-room apartment in the same building, where she lives today.

Dmitry was eager to show his grandmother the sights, anxious to demonstrate his new American ways. For a while he took Mrs. Byalskay everywhere, but gradually he became busy with school and his friends, especially Peter.

"I try to give her some attention, but there is so much I have to do."

Irina sees her mother every day. Their contact eases the loneliness.

Recently, Mrs. Byalskay began English study in a local school. Up until now, her daily conversation was only in Russian. In a class of immigrants from many other countries, she is the only one from Russia. Irina says proudly, "She is almost the best in the class already."

Mrs. Byalskay has adjusted quickly to some aspects of American life. She enjoys the television offerings of this country and has used a portion of her living allotment to buy a color television.

As to whether or not her mother is glad she came, Irina shrugs her shoulders. "It's hard to say. She doesn't blame me for bringing her."

For Dmitry, much of the struggle of arrival that his grandmother now suffers is fading. His days are no longer filled with jealous frustration in trying to understand what his deskmate's book says. In fact, English is Dmitry's favorite school subject.

Unhappiness has been replaced with excitement—
about school, about friends, about people.

"My school is small. There are only twenty in a class,
and most of the time we're split in two groups. With ten
in a group you get a chance to know everyone. Girls want
to sit next to me. I let them.

"It's friendly, but it's formal at the same time. There are
rules—no sneakers, no dungarees. Many boys wear
sports jackets. You must be clean, your hair must be
combed, and you must not have dandruff!

"People are beginning to invite me to parties. They
have good parties. The best one will be where there is one
boy for all the girls—I hope it's me," he jokes. "People are
beginning to think of me as just another kid, not the kid
from Russia."

FURTHER READING

Archer, Jules. *You Can't Do That to Me! Famous Fights for Human Rights.* New York: Macmillan, 1980.

Axelbank, Albert. *Soviet Dissent: Intellectuals, Jews and Detente.* New York: Watts, 1975.

Blue, Rose. *Cold Rain on the Water.* New York: McGraw-Hill, 1979.

Cavanah, Frances. *We Wanted to Be Free: The Stories of Refugees and Exiles in America.* Turbotville, Pennsylvania: Macrae, 1971.

Dornberg, John. *The Soviet Union Today.* New York: Dial, 1976.

Eubank, Nancy. *Russians in America.* Minneapolis: Lerner, 1973.

Forman, James D. *Communism: From Marx's* Manifesto *to 20th Century Reality.* 2nd ed. New York: Watts, 1979.

Hartmann, Edward. *American Immigration.* Minneapolis: Lerner, 1978.

Hewitt, Philip. *Looking at Russia.* New York: Lippincott, 1977.

Loescher, Gil, with Loescher, Ann. *Human Rights: A Global Crisis.* New York: Dutton, 1979.

Mann, Arthur. *Immigrants in American Life: Selected Readings.* Rev. ed. Boston: Houghton Mifflin, 1974.

Masey, Mary. *Picture Story of the Soviet Union.* New York: McKay, 1971.

May, Charles. *The Uprooted.* Philadelphia: Westminster, 1976.

Morey, George. *Soviet Union.* Morristown, New Jersey: Silver Burdett, 1976.

Morton, Miriam. *Pleasures and Palaces: After-School Activities of Russian Children.* New York: Atheneum, 1972.

Nazaroff, Alexander. *The Land and People of Russia.* Rev. ed. New York: Lippincott, 1972.

Snyder, Gerald. *Human Rights.* New York: Watts, 1980.

Snyder, Louis. *The Soviet Union.* 2nd rev. ed. New York: Watts, 1978.

Watson, Jane. *The Soviet Union: Land of Many Peoples.* Champaign, Illinois: Garrard, 1973.

INDEX